ABC of
Men's Fashion

ABC

OF MEN'S

FASHION

Hardy Amies

Abrams, New York

Cover design: Andrew Prinz
Production Manager: Anet Sirna-Bruder

Cataloging-in-Publication data has been applied
for and is available from the Library of Congress.
ISBN 13: 978-0-8109-9460-7
ISBN 10: 0-8109-9460-7

First published by Newnes, 1964
This edition published by Abrams, 2007

Printed and bound in China
10 9 8 7 6 5 4 3 2

Abrams books are available at special discounts when purchased in quantity for
premiums and promotions as well as fundraising or educational use. Special editions
can also be created to specification. For details, contact specialsales@abramsbooks.com
or the address below.

THE ART OF BOOKS SINCE 1949

115 West 18th Street
New York, NY 10011
www.abramsbooks.com

"A man should look as if he had bought his clothes with intelligence, put them on with care, and then forgotten all about them."

Introduction

To a privileged few, Sir Hardy Amies (1909–2003) seemed somewhat humble; to a great many others he was a wonderful snob with a wicked sense of humour. Over his long career as London's most successful couturier he was best known as dresser to HM Queen Elizabeth II from her accession to his retirement in 1989 – but his impact on fashion history has been far-reaching.

One of the founders of ready-to-wear clothing for men, Amies remarked that his designs looked equally good on an urban English gent or an American athlete. Certainly his customers agreed, and his clothes were worn by everyone from Lord Snowden and Peter Sellers to David Hockney and Ronald Reagan. In 1966, he designed for the England World Cup team, in particular its captain Bobby Moore. He also designed for the cinema, creating the futuristic – yet fashionable – costumes for Stanley Kubrick's *2001: A Space Odyssey*. He made the bowler hat fashionable again when dressing Patrick Macnee as the super spy John Steed in *The Avengers*.

Amies penned the *ABC of Men's Fashion* at a time when Savile Row was at the forefront of a great revival in men's tailoring. It quickly became a style bible for men, and indeed for women. Capturing Amies' icy cool nerves and expert knowledge, the *ABC* guides you through fashion's dangers and pitfalls, and addresses all that Hardy loved and loathed. The *ABC* still eloquently describes the Hardy Amies style, beautifully encapsulated by Amies himself: 'A man should look as if he had bought his clothes with intelligence, put them on with care and then forgotten all about them.'

Austin Mutti-Mewse
Curator, Hardy Amies Archive
London, 2009